STONER

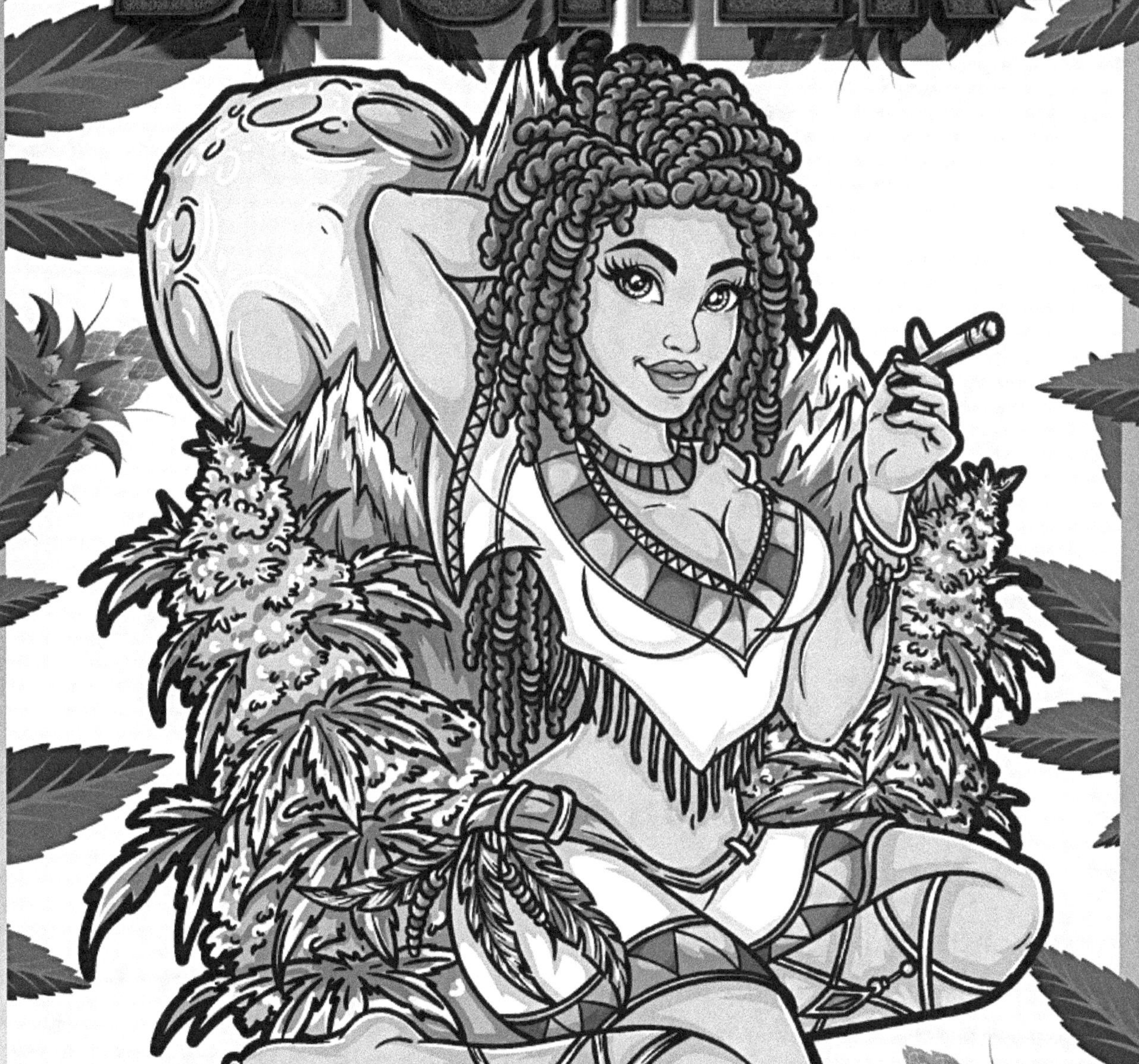

COLORING BOOK FOR ADULTS

+20 Psychedelic Mandala Bonus

STONER

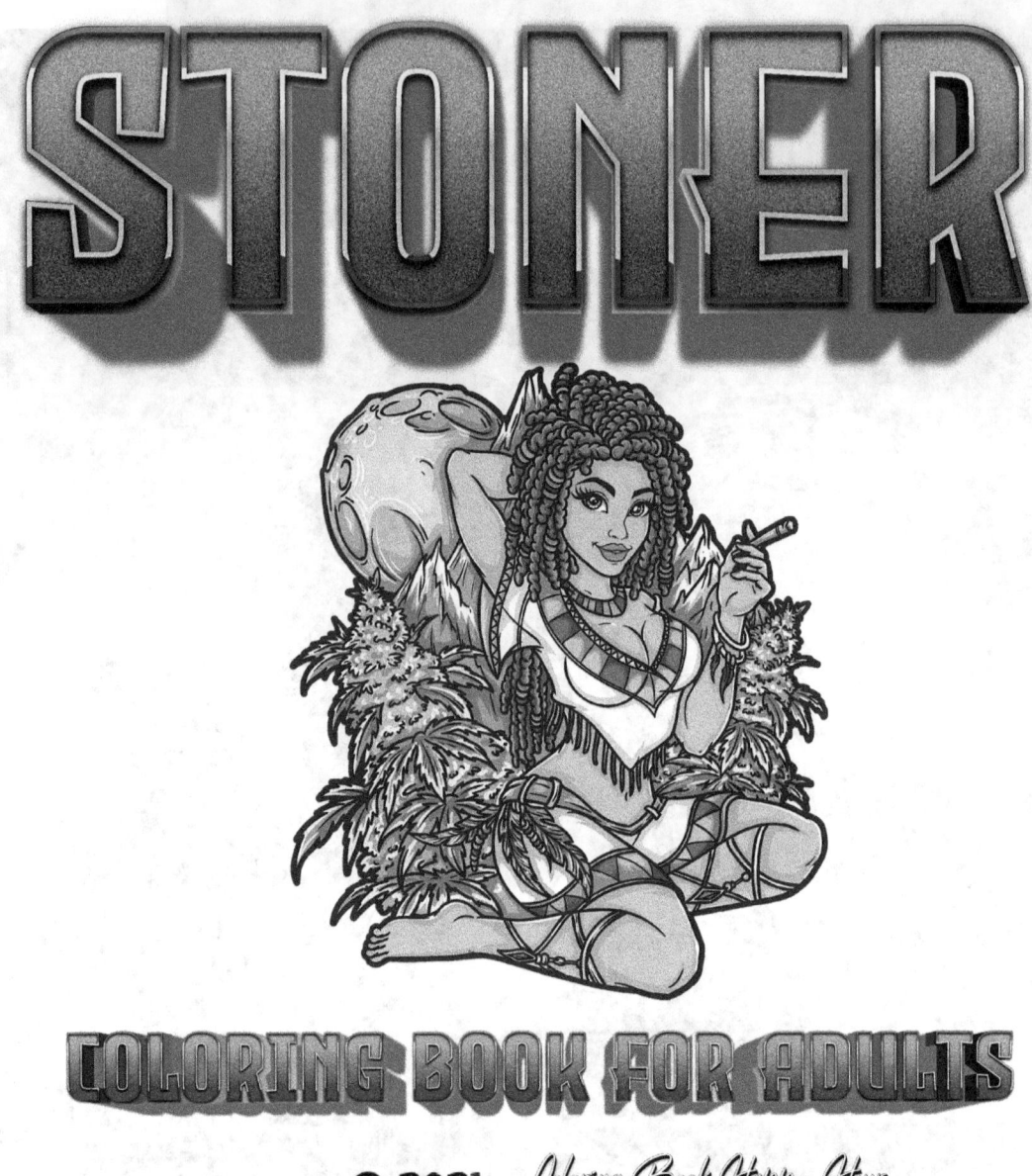

COLORING BOOK FOR ADULTS

© **2021** *- Coloring Book Happy Hour -*

All rights reserved.
No part of this publication may be reproduced, distributed or transmitted in any form or by any means including photocopying, recording or other electronic or mechanical methods without the prior written permission of the publisher, except in the case of brief quotations embodied in critical reviews and certain other non commercial uses permitted by copyright law.

Thank you for your recent purchase.

If you wouldn't mind leaving an online review section, we would really appreciate that. We love hearing everyone thoughts and comments.

THIS BOOK BELONGS TO

....

....

+20 Bonus

Mandala

Psychedelic

www.ingramcontent.com/pod-product-compliance
Lightning Source LLC
LaVergne TN
LVHW061946070526
838199LV00060B/4004